Sel   Selfridge, Oliver G.
             Trouble with dragons; pictures
           by Shirley Hughes. Addison, c1978.
           86p illus

             TITLE IV, PT. 3

           1 FAIRY TALES I Title

DATE DUE			
710 CM	OCT 10 '84		
307 HH	DEC 12 '84		
737 KS	JAN 23 '85		
216 Dm	FEB 2		
4KC	FEB 15		
4JC	OCT 2 2 2002		

TROUBLE WITH DRAGONS

OLIVER G. SELFRIDGE

Trouble With Dragons

Pictures by Shirley Hughes

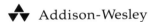 Addison-Wesley

Book designed by Charles Mikolaycak

Library of Congress Cataloging in Publication Data

Selfridge, Oliver G.
  Trouble with dragons.

  SUMMARY: Three sisters take turns at slaying a
dragon in order to win the hand of the prince.
    [1. Fairy tales] I. Hughes, Shirley. II. Title.
        PZ8.S3285Tr   [Fic]   77-22441
                         ISBN 0-201-07458-3

TROUBLE WITH DRAGONS

ONCE upon a time, long ago and far away, there was a beautiful kingdom by the sea, where everything was wonderful, except for the dragons. There was an old king and queen, who had two children, a princess and a prince. The princess had already fallen in love with a prince from a neighboring kingdom, and after a splendid banquet, she had gone to his home to help him rule. But alas! There was no princess for the young prince.

As you know, when a prince or princess goes out into the world to find a princess or prince, each one has to perform a difficult task, sometimes three difficult tasks. Some difficult tasks are more difficult than others, and generally they are a little dangerous too. To perform the difficult task a princess or prince usually has to be both brave and clever; it often helps to be lucky as well. One possible task might be to balance an elephant on the head of a pin. That is not as difficult as it might sound, though it involves being lucky enough to find either an extraordinarily small elephant or an extraordinarily large pin.

A harder task, perhaps nearly impossible, might be to move a mountain. Sometimes the princess or prince would hire thousands of people, with shovels and baskets and bulldozers and cranes, and so on. Perhaps they might move the mountain in time, if it was a small one, and perhaps not. Some difficult tasks seem to be really impossible. One prince was asked to cut a large meadow with a pair of nail scissors. As fast as he cut it, the grass grew up even taller. It is rumored that he is still inside the meadow, looking for a way out, for the grass has grown far above his head. It is possible that the prince should have used trickery or magic, but anyhow, he has never been seen since.

In another instance, a princess was asked to turn the whole ocean red, and eventually she thought of persuading her father to tell the dictionary makers to exchange the meanings of the words "red" and "blue." When new editions of the dictionaries had been published, therefore, the oceans were all red, and when the princess cut her hand by accident and looked at the blood, it was all blue, which is why we talk about princesses and dukes and lords and other aristocrats having blue blood. I suppose that that wasn't really a fair way to perform the task, but I don't know what else she could have done. However, that was unusual, and the more usual tasks were conquering wicked dukes or slaying dragons. Ah! Dragons! The kingdom didn't have many dragons, but those they did have were especially ferocious and angry and hard to deal with.

Dragons! Nobody knew where they came from; some say out of deep volcanic caverns, some say from mankind's wicked nature, and some say that dragons are a permanent necessary evil, terrifying and random, not to be understood or explained.

Dragons! The whole land would shake when one came out of the forest, whooshing fire and smoke through its nostrils, eating a whole herd of cows, or burning up a field of corn.

Dragons! The worst thing was that they needed to eat people, especially young maidens. Dragons needed to eat people in order to lay their sapphire eggs, from which were made the royal wine goblets. Other royal people and rich people in foreign countries could buy these magnificent goblets, which were extremely expensive. Most dragons lay ordinary eggs; there are said to be a few that lay porcelain ones, but only in this kingdom by the sea did dragons lay sapphire eggs. It might have had something to do with the fact that these were the only dragons in the world with blue eyes. As you know, sapphires are the best and most expensive blue gemstones there are.

I'm sorry to say that the Prime Minister of this kingdom was secretly quite a wicked man. He owned and ran the goblet factory, and he was always needing dragons' eggs from which to make goblets. Goblets sold for a lot of money indeed. So, the Prime Minister always hoped that the dragons would find more people to eat, especially maidens, because the blood of maidens made sapphire eggs of the very finest quality.

Now, the Prime Minister had the job of providing the young prince with a list of difficult tasks to give to visiting princesses. Recently the only thing that had been on those lists had been "Slay a dragon." The Prime Minister knew very well that slaying dragons was extremely dangerous. Beautiful and clever princesses would come to see the Prince, they would fall in love with him, they would go out and try to slay a dragon, and the dragon would eat them. Very sad! After a princess had been eaten, the Prime Minister would send his factory workers into the woods and the forests to pick up the dragon's eggs. Dragons don't take good care of their eggs, but just drop them in the underbrush around the forest.

The best way to slay a dragon is to ask a saint to come and slay it for you, like Saint George. But whenever the king wrote a letter to ask a saint for help in slaying a dragon, the Prime Minister would make sure that the letter was never mailed. He wanted the dragons to keep on laying their sapphire eggs from which he could make the royal sapphire goblets.

Meanwhile, the dragons did the most terrible damage, and several times a year, a beautiful and clever princess would come to visit the Prince. They would fall wildly in love — the Prince would give her a task of slaying a dragon — the princess would go bravely into the forest — and she would get eaten by the dragon. Alas!

That made the Prince very sad, as you might expect. And I daresay that the princesses who got eaten didn't enjoy it much either.

The Prince had been planning to go visiting other kingdoms, seeking a princess for himself, but then the old king and queen died, leaving him with the heavy burden of running the country by himself.

ONE day, on the road leading along the coast to the capital city, three coaches could be seen, piled high with baggage, bicycles, bonnets and bookcases brimful with books. Each coach was pulled by two white horses, and beside each driver a small flag displayed a discreet but authoritative crown, showing that the coach was a royal coach.

Far behind the coaches, three young princesses were having a picnic in a meadow next to the road. Their three horses were gently nibbling the meadow grasses. The princesses themselves were eating egg rolls and cold roast beef, and drinking red wine. They were all very clever and very beautiful, though of course very different from one another. They wore blue jeans and t-shirts because they all knew how hard it was to ride horses in crowns and royal robes. The t-shirts were each marked with a royal crest, so that commoners could easily tell that they were royal princesses.

As they were sitting there, enjoying their picnic, they looked up and saw a very old woman slowly hobbling down the road.

"Perhaps we should ask her to join us for lunch," said Celia, the youngest princess.

"I'm not sure she would be comfortable with us," said the eldest princess, whose name was Amanda.

"And first, we'd better make sure that there's enough food," added Belinda, the remaining princess.

Celia ignored her two sisters and called out, "Old lady, old lady! Won't you come and have some lunch with us? There's lots to eat."

The old woman looked up in some surprise and stopped hobbling.

"Why, thank you, my dears," she said in quite a strong voice. "Yes, I think that I will join you. It's extraordinarily kind of you." She strode briskly over to the picnic basket and sat down next to the three princesses, never stopping talking.

"My dears, this is really too kind of you for words." — although it seemed to be just kind enough for lots of words — "It's so dry and dusty, you have no idea. Here I am, a poor old fairy godmother, and I'm getting so old I forget to eat, and then before you know it, I'm almost *too* hungry to eat. Not exactly too hungry, but I get too hungry to think about eating. Until someone reminds me, someone nice, that is," and she kept on talking without saying very much. Finally she stopped to take a bite of chicken.

While she was eating, the eldest princess asked politely, "Are you anybody's in particular fairy godmother, or do you just go around being a fairy godmother to anyone who needs one?"

"Oh, no, my dear," said the fairy godmother, "that would be quite against the rules. They're very strict, you know. Let me see now. This century, I have to be a fairy godmother nineteen times. Right now, I'm fairy godmother to the young prince at the palace. You know, the one you're going to visit."

The princesses looked at each other. "Why, how did you know that?" asked Belinda.

"Just because I forget a lot," said the old lady, "doesn't mean that I don't still know a lot, at the same time."

"Won't you tell us about him, please?" said Celia, the third princess.

"Well, actually I haven't seen him in five years," she replied. "We got into a terrible fight at his fifteenth birthday party. He was really quite rude to me and said that I talked too much. Now, my dears, I know that I talk a lot — I'm nearly always talking — sometimes I think I'm almost never *not* talking — but that was not a polite thing to say, and I told him so, and he got quite angry. Can you imagine being angry at your fairy godmother? So I decided I wouldn't visit him until he apologized. And he hasn't yet."

"It's sad," she went on, "because of course he does need me. But we fairy godmothers have our pride. He's really a very nice prince. A little headstrong, a little thoughtless, that's all. Nothing truly objectionable. He always wants to go with the princesses to help them slay the dragons, but, of course, that is absolutely against the rules.

"I suppose you'll fall in love with him, you three," she said, "and each of you will get sent to slay a dragon." She gave a deep sigh and took a big sip of the crimson wine that accompanied the picnic lunch.

"Oh, no, we can't all fall in love with him," said Amanda, the first princess. "It's got to be me because I'm the eldest. He'll send me to slay a dragon, which, of course, I'll do easily because I'm brave and clever . . ."

"Boastful, too," said Belinda, but under her breath.

". . . and then the Prince and I will get married. You two," she turned to her sisters, "can stay a while and then

ride on to the next kingdom. Then, if Belinda can perform her task, Celia will have to ride on alone to another kingdom."

The fairy godmother said nothing at all. She held up the wine to the sun, and the sun shining through it made red lights move on her wrinkled face. She drank it down in one swallow and stood up.

"Thank you all very much," said the fairy godmother, "but I have to be hobbling along now. It was certainly very kind of you to have given me that delicious lunch."

She turned to Amanda, the eldest princess. "I should like to give you," she said, "three wishes. You may need them in your fight against the dragon."

The eldest princess looked a little embarrassed. "Oh no, thank you," she said, sounding a little pompous, "but I think using wishes against dragons wouldn't quite be the decent thing to do, you know. I ought to win only because I'm brave and clever."

"Well, it's just as you please," said the fairy godmother, and she didn't seem to take offense. She turned to Belinda, the next princess.

"My dear," she said, "I give you two free wishes. If you tell me what they are, I will grant them at once."

Belinda was at times far too clever for her own good, and this was one of those times. "Why, thank you, fairy godmother, I should like to use my first wish to change my second wish into two thousand wishes."

This time the old fairy godmother really did look offended.

"Certainly not!" she said. "That would be most improper. A form of wish cheating. No, we can't do anything like that. I'm most shocked. Who would have thought that a nice looking, intelligent, well brought up princess like you could have imagined such a thing? Why it's the most . . ." And she went on for a while.

Finally she turned to Celia, the third princess.

"My dear, I offer you one free wish."

Celia had been thinking furiously, so that she could avoid making the mistakes that her sisters had made.

"Thank you, fairy godmother," she said. "What I would really like would be for you to be fairy godmother for all three of us as well as for the Prince."

It was clearly the right thing to say. The fairy godmother smiled and smiled. "So be it," she said. She spun quickly around and ran back at full tilt to the road, where suddenly the princesses saw her hobbling along slowly just as before.

"What a funny old woman!" said Amanda.

"She talked so much," said Belinda.

"I wonder if she really is a fairy godmother," said Celia.

Anyhow, they packed up their picnic basket and tied it to the pommel of one of the saddles. Then they mounted their horses and rode off at a gallop after the coaches that held their baggage.

BY EVENING, the princesses were settled as guests at the
royal palace; they had nearly forgotten about the old lady
at the picnic.

The next morning, Amanda, the eldest princess,
went to visit the Prince. After a short time, they both fell
head over heels in love. Each thought that the other was
the most wonderful person there ever could be.

"You know," said the Prince, "that you have to go
and slay a dragon. I wish I could come, but it's against the
rules."

Princess Amanda laughed. "Nothing could keep me
from coming back to you with the head of a dragon drag-
ging behind my horse. I'll do it at once."

And she returned to her sisters to tell them the wonderful news, and also to oil her armor and to sharpen her
sword. She had to be properly ready for the fearsome
fight with the dragon.

In the meantime, the wicked Prime Minister had sent
a telegram to the goblet factory, which told the egg collec-
tors to be ready to go out into the forest to collect new
dragon eggs. He was sure that they would be laid after —
alas! — the dragon had eaten Amanda.

Her two sisters stayed up late that night talking and
wondering what was going to happen.

"I'm sure that it's very wrong of me," said Belinda,
"but part of me wishes that Amanda would get eaten up
by the dragon, so that I would have a chance."

"I know what you mean," said Celia, "and then I
think that, if Amanda gets eaten, maybe you will get
eaten, and there are all the other princesses that have
been eaten, so what chance would I have? There must be,
after all, a great many other princes and kingdoms in the

world. There must be one who wouldn't need a dragon slain."

In the morning, before the sun had risen or the cocks in the palace courtyard had crowed, even before the footmen had started to light the kitchen fires, Amanda arose and dressed herself in her dragon-fighting armor. The armor was exceedingly strong, made out of the very best steel; it was also very carefully lined with insulation, to guard against the flames and hot smoke that the dragon might breathe out.

"This is all pretty exciting," said Belinda.

"It's what we came for, after all," said Amanda, with a superior air. "You don't suppose that those courses on intermediate armor-polishing and advanced dragon-skinning were just to keep us busy.

"Now, Celia," Amanda continued rather pompously, "please make sure that my sword is sharp enough." Her sword was what she was proudest of.

Celia withdrew the shining steel blade from its scabbard. She set it on the table so that the sharpest part of the blade was uppermost. Then she took a handkerchief from her sleeve — so gossamer thin that you could see right through it.

She held it over the blade, about six inches up in the air, and let it fall. The handkerchief drifted down onto the sword, rested there a second, and then, almost with a sigh, fell into two parts on either side.

"It's sharp enough, your highness," said Celia, a little angry. "That's my sixth handkerchief this week, and you haven't used that sword yet."

"Oh, don't fuss," replied her sister. "One can't be too careful." All the preparations took quite some time, and by the time she was ready, the sun was angling into the courtyard.

"Yoicks!" cried Amanda in a low voice, and she galloped out of the palace courtyard.

Of course, no horse can keep up galloping for very long, especially with a heavy princess in full armor on its back, and round the first bend in the road, Amanda slowed the horse down to a walk. She had expected to be looked at as she rode through town, but the townspeople had seen dozens of princesses, always going just one way, so only an occasional child shouted, "Look, Ma! There's another one."

Amanda rode out of town on the main road. It wasn't until she reached the crossroads that she realized that she hadn't the slightest idea how to go about finding a dragon — let alone finding one that could be slain. She was puzzled, for there were three different roads that led more or less towards the band of forests that covered most of the horizon. After riding around the crossroads twice, she dismounted and sat down to have a bite to eat.

"I'll just ask the first person to come along."

As she was looking around, an owl drifted out of the nearby trees, gliding almost without moving a feather, and perched on the low fence beside her. The owl fitted its feathers together behind its back, as if warming them. And then, to Amanda's surprise, just as clear as clear, the owl spoke.

"I could tell you a thing or two."

Amanda sighed. "You must be magic," she said. "Owls don't talk ordinarily. But I was set this difficult task to do myself; it wouldn't be proper for magic to help me."

The owl looked back at Amanda and winked both eyes, one at a time. The owl was really the fairy godmother in a magic disguise, but of course, Amanda had no way of knowing that. "Well, you're consistent," it said. Its voice was thin and high, but very clear. As Amanda watched, it flew away with slow deliberate flaps to sit on the branch of a neighboring tree.

Presently, along the road from the town came a man pedaling on a tricycle. He was pulling quite a large wagon behind him loaded with goods. They seemed to be mostly food, some kegs of beer, a barrel of wine, great piles of potatoes and a side of beef.

The man stopped opposite Amanda.

"Good day, your highness," he said. He took off a rather ragged cap and swept it in front of him in a broad bow, while still seated on his tricycle.

"Good day to you, too," said Amanda, a little sternly. "You must tell me where to find dragons."

"Aye, your highness," replied the man. "Dragons may be found at the end of the center road, miles beyond where my inn is. For I am the Innkeeper. It's a far piece to where the dragons be," — he pronounced it 'fur piece,' — "and you'll need to be spending the night at my inn or else under the trees on spruce needles. Come, my boys will brush and curry your horse and feed him oats."

Amanda was a little puzzled. He seemed rather crafty, but she couldn't put her finger on what was wrong. She didn't really want to sleep in a field. She made up her mind.

"Thank you, Innkeeper. Yes, I should be delighted to accept your hospitality."

As the Innkeeper started pedaling again, going up the center road not very fast, Amanda climbed back on her horse with some difficulty, for her armor and sword and shield made her very heavy.

After a mile or so, the road left the pleasant meadows and entered a dark spruce forest where it began to twist and wind. There seemed to be nothing living in the forest, except an occasional owl; it was almost as if there was only one owl, flying through the black spruce trees, keeping up with the two travelers.

As the road grew steeper, the Innkeeper pedaled slower. After they had turned around a particularly steep corner, Amanda saw the inn, a long, low log cottage with a small barn at one end and a thin wisp of smoke coming

out of the chimney and disappearing amongst the dark
branches overhead. It was an unprepossessing sight. The
logs still had the bark on them, except for the patches
where it had fallen off. The cracks had been chinked with
moss and mud.

Amanda shivered. Dragon-hunting wasn't quite so
glamorous and exciting as she had imagined it would be.
In fact, she felt distinctly lonely.

The Innkeeper clapped his hands, and two boys came
running to take his tricycle and the princess's horse to the
barn. Then he took the princess into the inn, which was
dark and cheerless but warm. He ordered the cook, a sul-
len woman, to prepare a frugal meal for Amanda. He
turned to Amanda, "Princesses always eat frugal meals
before trying to slay dragons. And afterwards," he gave a
delicate little cough, "after the battle, the victor has a
victory banquet."

"That will be entirely satisfactory," said Amanda in a
haughty tone.

The frugal meal turned out to be a good frugal meal. Amanda had no wine to drink; her teacher had told her that, although drinking wine might increase her bravery, it could only diminish her skill and speed. After supper, the princess and the Innkeeper sat down by a blazing fire.

The Innkeeper told Amanda of the beauty and excitement of the dragons for a while.

"Have you slain many dragons, your highness?" asked the Innkeeper.

"No, this will be my very first one," said Amanda.

The Innkeeper spoke of nothing important, because he was thinking wicked thoughts and making wicked plans. He was thinking wicked thoughts, because he was a wicked person and secretly worked for the Prime Minister. He was in charge of the Collection Department of the Goblet Factory, as well as being the innkeeper. Collection didn't mean collection of money for overdue bills, as it does in other places, but collection of the sapphire eggs of the dragons. His stable boys worked in the forests for him, following the dragons' footprints stamped in the dead leaves and the underbrush, looking for the telltale glints of blue. They had to work fast because the footprints left by dragons filled in and vanished much faster than ordinary footprints, even though they were much larger indeed. That was why usually it took a lot of searching to find an egg; there was little of a trail to follow.

After supper, Amanda went directly to bed so that she would be well rested to fight the dragon. As she was about to climb in between the sheets, she heard a light tapping at the window. When she went over to see what it was, there was an owl, pecking at the window, as if motioning her to open it. "Another magic owl," thought Amanda. So she closed the shutters from the inside and went back to bed. If she had only known! For the truth is that that was no ordinary owl, but the fairy godmother trying to warn her of the dreadful danger she was in.

After breakfast the next morning, Amanda was drinking a cup of coffee while the Innkeeper hovered around, clearing the dishes and looking at her. Finally he sat down across the table and took out his pipe.

"Some people say, your highness," said the Innkeeper a little slyly, "that the reports of the damage dragons do are much exaggerated, very much exaggerated. Some do say that there's really no harm in them beasts, and of course, they do bring the tourists . . ."

Amanda was looking at him, astonished, but she didn't say anything. Encouraged, he went on.

"They are beautiful creatures, you must admit," he said shaking his head. "This morning, whatever you do, you must first come to the lookout. There, quite safely, you can often see a dragon, ramping through the forest alongside the craggy cliffs, its blue and red scales flashing in the dappled sunlight. Ah, they be a brave sight with the smoke snorting from their nostrils."

The Innkeeper paused for a moment and stirred the fire.

"I ween that dragons play their role in the balance of the forests. They aren't there for nothing. Some think the world would be worse off without dragons.

"Yes, perhaps the reports of the damage are a little exaggerated. I'm not saying for sure that they are, but it is a possibility, isn't it? If I were collecting insurance, I might easily be persuaded to exaggerate the damage myself, just for the insurance. It would be wrong, of course.

"Here now, your highness, I'll show you some pictures. They're much better than the usual postcards."

And he brought out a little album of the most wonderful photographs and paintings of dragons in various poses, doing various things, none apparently very harmful or dangerous.

Amanda seemed a little confused. She looked for a long while at a picture of a small dragon that seemed to be lost. "But," she said, "why would everyone say they're dangerous if they're not?"

"I'm sure I couldn't say. But it might have something to do with the insurance. As you know, I don't think dragons ever really mean to do harm. They're just following their nature. Perhaps what the kingdom needs is a kind of preserve, where dragons can be dragons. They're pretty rare now, you know. I think the world would be worse off if they became extinct."

Amanda began to sound distraught. "But I came here to slay a dragon. It's a task that has been given me. I can't go back to that wonderful prince in the palace without having slain a dragon."

The Innkeeper frowned sympathetically. "It's a terrible problem; one can never be sure about what's really the best thing to do. Here now, you wait here, for I have a special surprise to show you. I don't show it to everyone, you know."

The Innkeeper went to the door, snapped his fingers for a stable boy and told him to go and get the box just inside the stable doors. When the boy returned, he was carrying a wooden box, about two feet across, with several small holes in the lid. The boy put it on the floor in front of the princess.

"There now, your highness," said the Innkeeper, "I don't think he's very well."

The princess didn't know quite what to expect, but she opened the box and gave a drawn out "ooooooh!," for inside there was a small dragon, the size of a kitten. He didn't look very well, for his scales weren't bright and shiny, as in the pictures, but rather pale, as if they were covered over with a thin sheet of paper. In fact, as the wicked Innkeeper well knew, the baby dragon was just about to molt, which means to shed his skin, and to grow new skin with sparkling new scales. He wasn't truly sick at all.

Amanda didn't know that. "Why," she said, "he's beautiful. May I pick him up?"

"Yes, of course; his claws are a little sharp, but he's not old enough to breathe smoke and fire. Don't pick him up by his tummy for he may scratch, but give him a place on your hands to stand on. When he gets annoyed, his breath can be a little offensive; so be gentle."

Amanda picked him up carefully and held him to her chest.

"He's so dear."

"The trouble is that I think he needs his mother."

In fact, as the wicked Innkeeper well knew, the baby dragon's mother would have been as likely to eat the baby dragon as not. The baby dragon rubbed his head against the princess's neck, as if in delight at being held like that.

"Oh, he's wonderful!" she said softly. "How can we get him back to his mother?"

All thoughts of slaying a dragon had left the princess.

"Well," said the Innkeeper with an apparent indifference, "I was going to get one of the boys to leave it . . ."

"You're to do no such thing," said Amanda, as though she were in a position to give orders. "I shall be the one to return it. You must tell me where to take it."

"Do you think that's wise, your highness? After all . . ."

"Yes, you must do as I say," snapped Amanda, not accustomed to being questioned by anyone, let alone by innkeepers.

The Innkeeper dropped his head obediently and said, "I think this one's mother is in a cave by a tarn about half a mile from here, your highness. I'll show you the path."

As the princess stroked the dragon right behind his jaw, as if it were a puppy, the Innkeeper rubbed his hands together and smiled maliciously.

They walked slowly out of the courtyard, and the Innkeeper pointed out the path across the small stream. Amanda walked along it, carrying the baby dragon close; she was half wishing for a newspaper photographer.

After a while, the dark forest began to have a different smell, not the woody, peaty smell of spruce needles. Amanda didn't know what it was, but the baby dragon did. It was the smell of a real grown-up dragon. The baby dragon knew instinctively that grown-up dragons don't much care for baby dragons, except as food. It gave a squeal and a snort, jumped out of Amanda's arms and ran off on its hind legs into the undergrowth. Amanda got down on her hands and knees and looked.

"Come back at once, baby dragon! Come back, do you hear! I have to take you to your mother."

But it was too late. Moving as silently as a cloud, a large dragon had crept up behind the princess. Its monstrous jaws opened, its long and ferociously sharp teeth glistening. The dragon turned its head sideways, picked up Amanda, threw her into the air and swallowed her down with a single crunch, armor, sword and all. Her sword had not even been drawn from its scabbard.

The dragon strode away. Half a mile down the path, it dropped a splendid sapphire egg, which was picked up by a stable boy who had been sent out to look.

WHEN the news of Amanda's end reached the palace, the Prince and the two princesses were terribly sad; but the Prince was not much surprised — it had happened so often before. Belinda wasted no time in mourning for Amanda but went to see the Prince at once. When she was announced, he gave a deep sigh. When their eyes met, the Prince realized that this princess was even more beautiful than her sister had been. Belinda was actually a very fetching and clever princess.

It was with some reluctance that the Prince gave Belinda the task of slaying a dragon. "Now, don't you go getting yourself eaten," he said, a little fatuously.

"No fear," said Belinda confidently. She was sure that she could take care of any dragon there was. She walked back to the royal guest suite in a kind of daze. You might have thought there would have been a period of mourning for Amanda, but the thought never crossed Belinda's mind. She told Celia about the Prince. He was intelligent, handsome, hardworking, considerate, she said.

Belinda was quite confident. "When I have slain the dragon," she told Celia, "the Prince and I will get married. Then we will be king and queen. You can stay for a while, if you like, before going on to another kingdom."

Belinda spent most of that day cleaning and oiling her armor. Her sword was sharp, even sharper than Amanda's, she thought, and she carefully touched the hilt with two drops of oil, so that it wouldn't stick in the scabbard when she needed it.

The next morning, as the sun was beginning to light up the turrets of the palace, Belinda was all ready to go. She looked very efficient and powerful, sitting astride her horse as Celia led it to the palace gate.

"I hope there are enough dragons to choose from," said Belinda to Celia. "I should look pretty foolish if the only one I could find was too small. And it would be pretty risky to try to slay a dragon that was too big."

Celia said nothing but stood waving as Belinda rode off on her task.

Belinda rode out of the town just like Amanda, and like Amanda, it wasn't until she reached the crossroads that she realized she hadn't the slightest idea how to find a dragon.

"Although my sword is so sharp that it makes razors blush for their bluntness," she thought to herself, "it doesn't do me any good if I don't know which way to go.

"Still, I have to start somewhere. I can't spend all day here. Perhaps I can slay a dragon and be back at the palace in time for dinner."

And she chose the middle road among the three, riding a good deal faster than her sister had done. The middle road ran through meadows and clumps of woods, drawing closer to the line of dark forests on the horizon.

"That must be where the dragons live," thought Belinda. "I wonder how long it will take to find a satisfactory one."

At the next bend in the road, she heard a violent scuffling in the hedges lining the edge of the road. She dismounted and peered through the bushes. There was an owl on its back, trying, with its claws, to keep off a fox. But the owl seemed to be getting the worst of it.

"Help me, help me," Belinda heard it say in a clear thin voice. "Help me, and I'll tell you about the wicked Innkeeper."

Belinda thought fast. It must be a magic owl, who had been sent to help her, and who had fallen prey to a fox. Well!

"If I help you, owl, will you also tell me how to find and slay a dragon?"

The owl suddenly gave a vicious slashing with its talons, sending the fox back a couple of steps. The owl jumped off its back; it swung its wings, left and right, at the neck of the fox, which yelped, turned around, and ran off whining.

The owl seemed to gather itself together.

"The very idea," it said reproachfully, "laying down conditions like that. For someone so clever, you're stupid. You can't make bargains with magic owls, or magic anything for that matter. The way you princesses these days seem to want so much for so little. It must say something about bringing up and education, I suppose."

Still grumbling, the owl waddled slowly into the road, turned its back and gave a little leap that sent it high enough in the air for its wings to catch. It flew off towards the dark spruces ahead. Of course, you know that this was the same owl as before and was, in reality, the fairy godmother in disguise.

"I wonder," thought Belinda, not the tiniest bit abashed, "what it was going to tell me about the Innkeeper. At least I know there's something suspicious about him. Come to think of it, that means there is an inn, which is better than a bank of spruce needles."

Later in the day, Belinda arrived at the same dark inn that her sister Amanda had visited. The Innkeeper was delighted to see her, but she kept her distance from him, mindful of what the owl had said.

The following morning he brought her breakfast in the courtyard between the barn and the side of the inn, and as he was clearing away her dishes, he began the same speech that he had made to her sister, Amanda, but Belinda interrupted him.

"What nonsense!" she said sternly. "The Prince wouldn't have given me this difficult task if it weren't necessary. Of course, I'm going to slay a dragon."

The Innkeeper puffed on his pipe, not disturbed.

"Be your sword sharp, your highness?" he asked, pronouncing the word 'sharp' without any R in it.

"It certainly is," said Belinda proudly.

The Innkeeper looked at her dubiously. "I have a blade here," he said, "sharper than ingratitude and keener than enthusiasm. I'll wager mine has a better edge than yours."

The princess stood up, frowning. She looked very regal. "My blade is the sharpest in the whole world," she said.

And Belinda pulled her sword from the scabbard and showed it to the Innkeeper — hilt first, of course, because you must never point a sword at a person unless you mean to run him through with it.

"Aye," said the Innkeeper, "that do be sharp, but not so sharp as mine." He went back indoors and presently reappeared with another sword. It wasn't nearly so beautiful as Belinda's, but even she was forced to admit that it was pretty sharp.

The Innkeeper cunningly repeated, "I'll wager mine be sharper than yours."

He lifted a six-inch log onto a sawhorse, leaning against the wall of the courtyard. Swinging his sword around his head, he made a single stroke and sliced a thin, round piece, which fell free, off the end of the log.

"Now, your highness, let's see if your sword can do that. I'll go and make sure that your horse is ready for you."

And he took his sword and went back into the inn, shouting for the stable boys.

Even then, Belinda suspected nothing. She, too, went up to the log, spun her sword around her head and aimed a great blow at the log which the Innkeeper's sword had sliced so easily. Her sword also sliced easily halfway through the log; then, with a jarring clank, it stuck firm and fast. Belinda was appalled. "What have I done?" she

said to herself. There was her beautiful sword stuck in a mere six-inch log.

"Innkeeper!" she shouted. "Innkeeper!"

There was no reply. You have probably guessed that the Innkeeper and the stable boys were scurrying away into the forest, leaving the princess weaponless against the dragons. Even then, Belinda didn't really realize what had happened. She began to put her whole strength into pulling her sword out of the log.

At this moment, a small dragon came right into the courtyard, moving swiftly and silently. And observing the princess, who in any case had no weapon at all, it ate her with two crunches, armor and all — except for the sword.

Sitting on the chimney, the owl shook its head sadly and flew off.

The dragon, full of fresh princess's blood, stomped around the courtyard and then ramped off into the forest to lay its sapphire eggs in the underbrush.

Later that afternoon, when the reporters arrived from the capital to write their stories about Belinda's being eaten by the dragon, the wicked Innkeeper told them a lot of lies. He showed them poor Belinda's sword — which had been stuck between nails he had driven into the log — and he told them he had seen the sword dented and broken on the dragon's tough and scaly hide. And that dented sword, once so sharp and beautiful, was all that was left of Belinda. He declared that the fight had taken place in a stony valley a mile away, and the photographers took pictures of it. He had been up in the lookout, sweeping it out, he said, when he saw Belinda "striding brave as brave towards the dragon. But it was too large and ferocious for her. Dragons do be fierce."

The newspapers the next morning showed pictures of the valley and the sword, and described the Innkeeper as being distraught at his guest's having been eaten. "It'll be terrible for the trade," he was quoted as saying.

But what the reporters didn't write, because they didn't know, was that by the very next morning, the Innkeeper and his stable boys had already found three sapphire eggs near the inn — and they expected to find a dozen more.

NEXT morning at the palace, Celia, who had heard the news and been much saddened by it, went to comfort the Prince. The Prince, it must be said, was in a real state. Celia and the Prince looked at each other.

"It's no good," he told her. "I'll never find a bride this way. You must be Celia. We'll fall in love; I'll have to send you to slay a dragon, and you'll get eaten too. And I'll still be miserable.

"I won't have it," he went on. "It's not fair. I think I won't marry. I'll stay a bachelor Prince all my life so that no more princesses have to die."

"Don't worry," said Celia, who was feeling brave and frightened at the same time. "Don't worry. I'll go and slay my dragon very carefully, and then we can get married, you and I."

"What makes you think that you'll do better than the others?" asked the Prince. "All the princesses have

thought they were going to do better than the previous ones."

The Prince wished that he had not offended his fairy godmother five years before. In difficult problems like this, fairy godmothers could be invaluable. He gloomily told Celia that he wouldn't give her a task of slaying a dragon. But she insisted, and with a heavy heart, the Prince did what she insisted.

Celia returned thoughtfully to her beautiful bedroom in the west tower of the palace. She sat at the window, thinking hard. She was pretty sure that she didn't want to be eaten up by a dragon — more than pretty sure, she was absolutely convinced.

"One trouble is," she said to herself, "that a princess who gets eaten up by a dragon can't tell anyone what went wrong. So the next princess, which is me, is just as likely to make the same mistakes and get eaten up, too. I wish I knew what really happened to the other princesses, especially my two sisters."

At that moment, there was a fluttering and a rustling. A large owl flew in the window and perched on the back of a chair, ruffling its feathers and stretching its neck left and right.

It spoke. "It's funny you should ask, for that's exactly what I've come to tell you."

Celia was at first taken aback, but she gathered her good sense, and her good manners, too.

"Oh, how do you do, owl! Can I send for something for you to eat or drink?" She wasn't at all sure what an owl might like to eat or drink, or whether the palace would have it.

"Well, my dear, I don't think I need anything right at this very minute." The owl walked unsteadily along the back of the chair, and Celia with a start realized that it must be her fairy godmother in disguise.

"Now I can't stay long, my dear, and so I'll just give you a brief picture. After it's all over, perhaps we'll have time to fill in the details." The owl proceeded to tell Celia about the wickedness that had gone on, resulting in her two sisters' being devoured by dragons.

Celia was appalled — and very angry at the Prime Minister. "I'll cut his head off; I'll have him drawn and quartered, or fifthed — whichever is more painful. And the Innkeeper — why he should be thrown to the dragons himself."

But the owl warned her that the unsupported word of an owl would not be regarded as enough justification for the kind of slaughter she was talking about.

"You have to have some reason that you know for yourself. Even a princess can't go around killing everybody, or else she would be thought a wicked tyrant.

"You have to know things and do brave and clever things for yourself. We fairy godmothers have to leave quite a lot undone and unsaid. So, the things we do and say are sometimes hard to understand or filled with double meanings.

"Now, you know that you will have to be more careful than the other princesses. They went off without knowing as much as they could about what they were up against.

"Remember, a sword won't make a person fall in love. Love is precious little good, fighting against magic. For each struggle, one must bring not only bravery and understanding, but also the right weapons. I also remind you that common or garden dragons don't lay sapphire eggs."

The owl spread out its wings experimentally, as if ready to take off. Celia thought, frowning a little. "Do you mean," she asked, "that perhaps the dragons are magic dragons, and that it is not quite enough merely to have a sharp sword and courage?"

The owl said nothing, but hopped to the window. It turned its head around, very slowly winked one eye and then the other. Then it jumped out into the air, and Celia heard only two rustling flaps before it was gone.

"Come to think of it," thought Celia, "what they told us in school about dragons was really pretty vague and simple. Perhaps I had better find out some more about these particular dragons and about this particular kingdom they infest. I wonder if there is a library here?"

The palace library did not show much sign of use, and the librarian seemed to be surprised that a real princess would come to use it.

"Usually they just send a servant, and we talk together, and I give them a nice illustrated picture of a dragon, showing which end is which. Then they go back to their princesses, and everybody is happy," he thought.

"Where do I look up dragons?" Celia asked the librarian.

"Under the letter D, your highness," he replied. "The cards are in the cabinet over there."

He showed her where they were. "Let me see," he continued. "Dragons would be mostly natural history, I should think. Perhaps some dragons would be unnatural history, but they would be filed in the same file, probably. Yes, here we are."

There weren't very many cards about dragons. The librarian felt that he ought to apologize. "You see, your highness, they're so exceedingly dangerous, it's hard to get close enough to study them. Scientists are sure they return to their caves in the mountains to die — if they ever do die — but, really, we don't know. It's just a guess. Most of the books and papers here are about the damage

they've done, the people and princesses they've eaten," he went on, a little absentmindedly, "the farms they've crashed through, the orchards they've scorched with their fiery and abominably poisonous breath.

"A few people have managed to take photographs of them. The Innkeeper up in the forest has taken several . . ."

"Yes, I've heard of him; I'll bet he has," said Celia sternly.

". . . good ones, but they don't show much. None of the ones in this kingdom has ever been slain."

"What I ought to do now," said Celia, "is to read all of these, even if they don't seem to be helpful. I'll do it right here and now."

"Very well, your highness, I'll bring them all to you here."

And he went off.

THE first book he brought was the *Royal Archives*, which had been started a hundred years ago. It contained records of all the times the dragons had been seen, and the times the dragons had wrought their damage to the countryside and its inhabitants. Celia turned the pages gloomily. They were too full — each handwritten entry meaning a family had lost something terribly important, like a father or a herd of cattle or a house.

The last two entries sent the tears rolling down her cheeks:

> *TUESDAY:* Pursuant to the duly assigned Royal Task 3A on the above date, the Royal Princess Amanda set forth, armed, along the middle road to the Dark Forest, vowing not to return until She had slain a dragon. It was then reported by the Innkeeper that She was Herself slain and devoured by a dragon shortly after She had bravely started out towards the mountains the next morning. This entry has been duly entered and signed by
>
> The Royal Record-Keeper

> *FRIDAY:* Pursuant to the duly assigned Royal Task 4A on the above date, the Royal Princess Belinda set forth, armed, along the middle road to the Dark Forest, vowing not to return until She had slain a dragon. It was then reported by the Innkeeper that She was Herself slain and devoured by a dragon. It was also reported that the Princess put up a brave fight, and Her sword, the sole remnant, has been duly entered

into the Royal Dragon Repository. This entry
has been duly entered and signed by
The Royal Record-Keeper

"If I'm not extraordinarily careful," thought Celia, "I 45
know what the next entry will be. I'd better have a look at
the sword, too, in a little while."

It was very interesting that nobody had ever actually
observed anyone's being eaten by a dragon. There was no
doubt that many people *had* been eaten, most taken by
surprise. One interesting case had happened many years
before.

A group of deer hunters had been creeping through
the brush. The sounds of a scuffle at the end of the group
had led two of the other hunters to whisper, "shhh!"
When one of them turned around, all she saw was a dragon striding away, leaving only the hunter's red cap on
the ground. Since then, there had been very few hunters.
Indeed, there had been very few deer seen in the dark forest. They had moved to the more open woods nearer the
coast; perhaps they had been driven away by the dragons.

That entry emphasized a curious fact. Dragons can
move extraordinarily silently and yet leave enormous
prints in the dirt and the underbrush. Even the poisonous
breathing is absolutely silent, unless flame is being emit-
ted — then there is a terrifying roar. But the stamp of the
footprints vanishes within a few minutes, even those two
or three feet deep.

Celia began to read the other books as they arrived.
Almost nothing was *really* known about dragons — what
they were made of, how they lived, where they came
from. Nobody had ever found a dead dragon. Doctors
declared that they couldn't be made of flesh, for no flesh
could stand the fierce heat of their flaming breath. And
could flesh make eggs of sapphire?

Not many people lived in the dark forest, and those who did had not written about dragons. The farmers had reported the damage they did, but they knew little else about them. Not many of the farmers went into the forest; when they did, it was only to collect firewood.

Behind the forest, the mountains had dark places and caves that had never been explored, and on cold quiet nights when sound travels well, farmers could sometimes hear roars rolling down the slopes and see flames flickering off the snowy peaks.

The third book had some good drawings. One showed a dragon pinning a cow beneath a claw. The cow was piteously mooing, while the nostrils of the dragon ejected a twelve-foot-long trumpet of fire and smoke. The dragon's scales were blue, except for a collar of red scales which extended halfway down the monster's back. The caption noted that the drawing had been made by a farmer, who watched helplessly from the top of a cliff while the dragon killed his whole herd of cattle.

The text explained that the farmer had pushed his iron wheelbarrow from the cliff, hoping to strike the dragon, when it passed far below. The wheelbarrow had, indeed, hit the dragon, and the clanging had echoed around the hills, but the dragon had seemed not to notice. The wheelbarrow itself was battered into uselessness.

The dragon in the drawing was about forty feet long, including its scaly blue tail. Its open jaws displayed rows of long sharp teeth which pointed backwards; so that prey once seized could never escape, but could only slide inexorably down the long throat.

"It seems to me," thought Celia, "that even a sharp sword won't do much good." She looked carefully through the cards again. Perhaps Saint George had written a little book called *Dragon Slaying — Professional Secrets of the Trade,* or something like that.

But there wasn't anything like that. Some of the books described dragons in other lands, but they seemed to be different. Some of them were smaller and had wings. Others were only called dragons, but were really just large lizards which any agile person could kill, and whose meat was supposed to be tasty.

"I don't need to know about other dragons," thought Celia, "especially if they are different from the ones here."

Some dragon watchers thought that dragons appeared less often in the winter, though perhaps they did more damage when they did appear then. Others claimed that dragon watchers simply watched a good deal less in winter. Dragons never ventured far from the dark forest, so that only the farms next to it were in much danger. The trouble was that the farmers in those farms would abandon them. Rather than be eaten by the dragons, they would buy farms further away or else move with their families into a town. Then their old farms would grow up into spruce forests, and the dark forest would grow larger; soon the farms *next to* the old farms would be in danger.

One might have thought that the dragons, rampaging through the forest, would have knocked down great trails — they were certainly large enough to push down any tree they wanted to. But no, they wove their wicked ways amongst the gloomy spruces without harming any, while orchards in full bloom at the end of May might be totally crushed and shattered.

THERE were several government pamphlets advising people to stay out of the "Northern Forests where dragons are scarce but exceedingly dangerous." If travelers wanted to see dragons, they should "take an official tour with an authorized guide who will lead you, in perfect safety, to the approved lookouts." Scientists and other observers were warned to stay clear as well. In fact, there had been no "official tours" during the last few years. Apparently visitors were more afraid of the dragons than they were curious about them.

Celia sighed. There were no clues to what dragons were vulnerable to. Nothing was known that would be any help to her in slaying a dragon. There weren't even any ideas about it. In her country, she felt, things would have been different. Every child would have wanted to learn about dragons, or at least see one, even if every parent had forbidden it. There would have been contests for seventh graders for the best and most imaginative essay on "How To Deal With The Dragon Scourge," or "Where Dragons Come From."

There was little enough, too, about the eggs and the goblet factory. There ought to have been a history of the goblet factory: who first dared go into the forest and took an egg; who made the first goblet. But nothing. The only worthwhile item was a map of the forest region, showing both the inn and the factory, which was only a mile or so away. The forest area was mostly blank on the map, except for a few trails with question marks beside them. "I suppose that means no one is sure exactly where the trails are," thought Celia.

She copied the map as best she could and returned the books to the librarian. At the Royal Dragon Repository, which was next door, Celia looked at her sister's sword. There was the huge nick from the nails in the log, just as the fairy godmother had described. The Innkeeper had added a few extra dents himself.

There were some other interesting things. The wheelbarrow that had been dropped on a dragon was there, very battered. Where it had struck the dragon, corrosion had eaten away the metal into a thin and fragile shell of rust. Then there were plaques for each of the princesses who had come seeking the hand of the Prince, but those for Amanda and Belinda had not been put up yet. There was also a single sapphire egg, too flawed to make into goblets, mounted next to a cluster of lights that made it sparkle like a luminous eye; it seemed to be watching Celia wherever she stood.

The Repository was more than a little depressing, ʻ
and the dust was thick. Not many visitors, clearly!

AS she left the Repository, Celia was thinking that she
had better bring a lance with her, as well as her sword.
Her professors had told her that lances were more of a
handicap than a help in a forest. Their size made it difficult to maneuver them through the trees. But there were
several ways to use a lance, and it would be safer to have
one and not need it than the other way around.

Celia returned to her rooms in the palace, and she ate
her supper there. It would not have been fitting for her to
eat in the main dining room, for she had officially under-
taken her task and could not return until she had accomplished it — or failed. As she sat at her table, studying the
map she had copied in the library, the Prime Minister,
who was working at a desk in a window across the courtyard, looked up and saw her radiant beauty with some
surprise.

THE Prime Minister was surprised because he had expected Celia to start off to slay a dragon at once, like her sisters. He was anticipating even more sapphire eggs, which would make his reserves comfortably large.

On weekends he would sometimes visit his small factory in the forest where the eggs were made into goblets. Each egg was picked up from the forest floor and rushed back to the factory where it was very carefully sliced in half. Sapphire is a very hard gemstone, but diamonds are even harder. There was one workman whose only job was to keep a small wheel tipped with many, very tiny diamonds, so that he could slice the eggs properly. A stable boy turned a crank, which pulled a belt, which turned the diamond wheel very fast. The egg, cradled at each end by silk pads, would rotate very gently, against the diamond wheel. Thus, a thin groove would be cut into the sapphire, right around the middle.

Then, the workman would look at that groove with a magnifying glass to find out the quality of that particular egg and to decide whether it should be Grade 1, 2 or 3. Sometimes an egg would have flaws, visible to the naked eye, that looked like patches or grainy pieces in the otherwise smooth azure. Such an egg might have been laid by a dragon suffering from some sickness, the way fingernails often show white streaks after sickness or an accident. Such an egg could not be made into a goblet for it would break at the flaw. Instead, it was boiled well — to make sure that the baby dragon would not hatch — and then polished, wrapped and boxed for sale as a conversation piece for some rich person's coffee table. The groove would be covered with a crimson ribbon around the middle of the egg.

But usually the egg looked flawless, and the workman went on to inspect the kind of layering in the groove, in order to decide whether the sapphire was thick enough and cohesive enough to stand the rest of the work that the best goblets needed. If it was of the highest quality, he would label it — two labels, one at each end, of course — with a small golden crown, and it would be sold only to royalty. Grades 2 and 3 were labeled with crimson numbers, and they would be sold to anyone rich enough to pay for them.

Finally, the workman would finish slicing the eggshell in two with the spinning diamond wheel. Under the sapphire shell was a toughish stuff like sausage skin or plastic; it held the contents of the egg, which were already turning into a baby dragon, the faster so because of the heat of his workshop. The workman would just dump the contents into a bucket, to be thrown away. The Prime Minister had tried to hatch a dragon himself once, but two things went wrong. First, baby dragons are sometimes dangerous because their breath can be poisonous. Second, the powerful corrosion of the developing dragon ruined the sapphire eggshell; by the natural time of hatching, the shell was as thin as a stocking and had lost its color, beauty and strength. It could be easily crumpled up. In fact, dragons don't need to have pipping teeth,* because their eggshells tear easily when they are ready.

After the two halves had been separated and cleaned, another workman glued golden stems to the ends. He would twirl each goblet in his fingers to make sure that the stem was properly centered. Then, more diamond

---

*Many kinds of birds grow pipping teeth while they are in their shells. Pipping teeth are small hard lumps on their foreheads or bills which hatching birds use to break their shells. After the hatching, the pipping tooth falls off. A pipping tooth is not a true tooth, and in any case, birds don't have true teeth at all. One of the meanings of the word "pip" is "to break through the shell (of a hatching bird)."

wheels ground the lip of the goblet smooth. Sometimes jewels were inlaid into the gold bases. Privately, the Prime Minister thought that was a little vulgar; still — if people wanted to pay for it, he would have it done for them.

The Prime Minister worried occasionally that his men would find all the eggs the dragons laid; then there would be no more dragons, and hence, no more dragons' eggs. But the number of dragons didn't seem to change. Perhaps the baby dragons were usually eaten by their parents anyway. The Prime Minister didn't worry about that at all. Part of wickedness lies in being concerned only about the things that are valuable to you. Enough eggs to keep the Prime Minister rich and to make him even richer — that was all he cared about.

The Innkeeper really knew quite a lot about the dragons and their lives, certainly more than the wicked Prime Minister knew. For example, he knew how to hatch a dragon from a badly flawed egg, and sometimes he would steal such an egg from the factory and let it hatch. He had discovered that the wood of the rowan tree, or mountain ash, was magically impervious to the poisonous breath of dragons. So he would build a small box of that wood, like the one he showed Amanda, and put the

egg in it. When it hatched, he would feed the baby dragon, already active and hungry, with small animals from the forest and with pieces of waste meat from the kitchen. He would mix mistletoe* with the meat. The mistletoe helped to keep the dragon docile and in good health until it grew too big (and it grew very quickly) for its box. The Innkeeper would then have his boys carry the box up into the mountains, build a bonfire and place the box next to it. When the fire set the box alight, the dragon would come out unharmed, for dragons seem to be at home with fire.

The Innkeeper never told anybody about this. He knew people would be angry if they found out he had raised a dragon to lay more eggs, ravage farmhouses and devour princesses and any other people who happened to be in its path.

The Prime Minister tried to make all his workmen keep track of how and where they found the eggs, which ones turned out best, and so on. He ordered them to write everything down, so that he could study what they said and see how to get better eggs and make better goblets. Now, the workmen were pretty careless about all of that and often made up things; what they wrote had little to do with the truth.

For example, the stable boys all knew of likely finding places which they never told one another and certainly never wrote down, for each one who found an egg was rewarded with extra money. Sometimes the less successful boys would spy on the more successful ones to see where they found eggs; then fights would break out, and they would return to the factory or to the inn with bloody noses and scrapes.

---

*Mistletoe seems to be magic too, remaining green and alive against the dull olive of the gloomy spruces when the snow lies deepest and the sun is sinking towards the nether regions.

The Prime Minister knew little of such matters. He would stroll through the factory, encouraging those who were working hard and scolding those who were not. He would read the records, largely filled with imaginary data; then he would walk quietly through the warehouse, where dozens of goblets lay packed in silk and dried rose petals. He would pull out a scented applewood casket, open it and blow aside the rose petals. They would rise in a pink and yellow cloud, then settle down around the casket and on the floor. He would lift out a goblet, and the beauty would give his heart the only warmth it ever felt. He would wish he could capture within him that warmth which, in people not so wicked as he was, comes from beauty in each other's hearts.

Then he would replace the goblet and leave with a scowl because his heart had grown cold and chill again. The factory workers knew better than to stay around him, for he was angry and would snap and snarl at them.

THE next morning, the Prime Minister stood in the palace window and watched Celia, preparing her horse and talking to the palace guard who was helping her. He felt some of her beauty too, and he wished that she would hurry away and be eaten by a dragon — quickly.

FROM high up on the palace tower, the fairy godmother watched Celia's preparations with mixed feelings. She was disguised as a beetle or a shadow or perhaps as a palace clock. Celia had clearly done better than previous princesses, though not quite well enough; she had missed a crucial part of the instructions. The fairy godmother thought it over for a while, and then decided not to interfere. Below, Celia had finished loading her horse and was climbing into the saddle. She would have liked to have told the Prince what she had done, then he would have wished her good luck. But they were forbidden to see each other until she had accomplished her task.

As she sat there, adjusting her helmet with its royal plume and resting her shield across her knees — its splendid red and blue surrounding the golden crown — she was well aware that she made a glorious picture. For a moment she had a great deal of sympathy for her sister, Amanda, who had always been very conscious of the photographers.

Celia rode slowly out of the courtyard, looking at the map that she had copied in the library. She glanced up at the tower of the palace and noticed the flag at half-mast. "Why," she thought, "that's for Amanda and Belinda. How easily I forget them! I hardly even mourned. But at least I am avenging them as much as I am winning a prince." She shuddered at the notion that perhaps there would be no vengeance and no winning, but just a crunch.

"If dragons are evil magic, probably the ordinary kinds of fighting won't help much," she mused, while her horse walked slowly through the town and out towards the crossroads. "Even the sharpest sword can't cut

through nails or granite. Even if I know more about dragons than my sisters, I don't really have any good ideas
about how to slay one."

She went on musing, "Perhaps the most important
thing is not to do the things that my sisters did." And
when she reached the crossroads, instead of taking the
middle road straight up towards the ring of dark forest,
she turned to the right. She rode slowly for a while. The
road veered slightly away from the forest, passing farms
and fields where farmers were cutting hay and spreading
it out to dry. Then the road forked, and she took the fork
on the left, which bore slightly uphill and headed back
towards the forest.

"I'd better keep a good lookout around me," she
thought. "Dragons can move so quietly."

The fields became more unkempt, and as the road
climbed slowly, patches of dark spruces appeared in the
hedges and coalesced until they reached far overhead and
began to block the sky. At the same time, as if that weren't
enough, the clouds, which had been patchy and summery
over the meadows, became bigger and grayer, and grew
together like the patches of spruce, until the sky itself was
gray and threatening.

The ground became rougher, too, with hillocks and
hummocks through which the path wound and twisted,
so that one couldn't see very far along it. The path dipped
into a hollow, and Celia crossed over a small clear river
flowing between muddy banks; the bridge was old, and it
creaked as her horse trod confidently along its length.
Further up the stream, next to a noisy little waterfall, a
man standing in the shallows was reaching up to the
overhanging branches and picking something, which he
would put in a basket on his back. Celia waved, but the
man didn't notice her, probably because of the noise of
the waterfall. She felt a little drizzle on her cheeks as the
sky was briefly visible.

After she had re-entered the forest, Celia realized that her sisters must have felt as lonely and scared as she did. She turned with a bend in the path, but the bridge was already out of sight. An owl hooted — a dismal sound, thought Celia.

Then a cheerful patch of blue appeared ahead, high up in the trees, and Celia thought, "Ah, the clouds are breaking; the sun will be a good deal more cheerful." The owl hooted again, sounding almost urgent, and Celia noticed with horror that the patch of blue seemed to be moving swiftly *through* the trees and towards her.

Celia reined her horse and sat still. The forest was absolutely silent, and the blue patches were still gliding high up across in front of her. Then a hundred yards ahead, round a bend in the path, the dragon appeared, almost luminously blue, monstrous and huge, taking deliberate strides, each half a dozen yards long. It must have been forty feet high, and it threaded its head among the branches with its vicious teeth gleaming in its open jaws and its blue eyes shining like stars.

This was not the place to fight a dragon, Celia decided instantly, especially one as big as this. Her horse was loaded down with baggage, and there was no room to dodge, to dart in and thrust at the beast, then to skip away and to return from the other side. She had not assembled her big lance; the pieces were still strapped together behind her. She whirled her horse around, thinking that the bridge across the stream might afford some safety. Her horse seemed to be anxious, too, and galloped without being urged to. But a princess in full armor, with baggage as well, is a heavy load. It was going to be a close race.

There is something about running away that makes anxiety swell into fear, and fear swell into panic. Looking over her shoulder, Celia was appalled at how quickly the dragon gained on her. Her horse's hooves thumped on the

wooden planks of the bridge, and the bridge shook as the first leg of the dragon landed. Celia felt the bridge give way beneath her. She looked back and up at the monster as its foot plunged right through the bridge, and it began to fall to one side. Its nostrils gave forth twin jets of dark brown smoke with a roar. Celia's horse was scrabbling up an ever steeper surface as the bridge sagged steadily into the river, but Celia was fascinated as the dragon toppled faster and faster to one side until it struck the muddy bank with its flank. Its long tail twitched around the sky, and the ultimate tip of it flicked across Celia, striking her on the forehead, knocking her quite clear of her horse and into the water.

She was completely stunned as her horse struck out for the bank. She couldn't see the dragon contort itself upright and move off back into the forest as steadily and silently as before.

Luckily the river was not deep, so that when the icy water had revived Celia, she stood up with her head and shoulders above the surface, coughing up water and tasting the saltiness of her own blood, which was dribbling steadily down from the middle of her forehead.

"Well, I'm lucky to be alive," she said to herself, as she stumbled towards the bank. She felt a helpful arm grip her elbow and support her shorewards. It was the man she had seen before; he was old and seemed kind.

"There, there, sit still. What on earth are you doing in all that tin? You might have drowned. That's a nasty gash you have on your forehead, but I'll wipe it clean."

He spoke gently and reassuringly. "Come we'll put you on your horse and take you to our shack; it's comfortable enough."

IT WAS a small log cabin with but a single window. Inside, there were a warm fire, a table, two bunks and some stools and a chair. Next to the window a wrinkled woman was standing, turning the crank on a small mill; the hopper dribbled gray fragments through the upper grindstone.

Celia was led to the fireplace and seated on a low stool. The old man watched as Celia slowly extricated herself from her armor. As each piece was laid down, he would wipe it dry and hang it from a row of nails in the wall by the fireplace. Her sollerets, which are the flexible steel shoes of a suit of armor, were full of water and mud. Then her feet began to warm themselves, and her stockings steamed in front of the fire.

"You've caught yourself a scar up there," said the woman sympathetically. The old man looked over and nodded.

"She's that lucky; it was but the tip of the tail. The beast broke the bridge; it's all ruined. It was the same big one. But once this girl was in the water, it didn't seem to notice her. She's lucky that a headache is all that'll happen." He glanced at the stack of kindling next to the stove and went outside.

"You wait there," said the woman, "and my man will fetch you a little stew with some pancakes on the side. It'll put you to feeling right. They're acorn pancakes.

"Acorns make good flour," the old woman continued. "You have to remember to boil them a couple of times to get the bitterness out of them. Then dry the mash in the sun and grind it fine. When you collect acorns, be sure to leave some for the forest; you don't have to worry about the squirrels — they will have taken their share already. That's what I'm doing now, grinding the acorn mash we put out to dry last week."

The old man entered with a load of wood, which he stacked by the fireplace. Without a word, he filled a plate at the stove and brought it to Celia. He put more wood on the fire.

"I've not finished yet," he said, and went out. After he had left, the princess devoured the good food with a glass of cool water. Then she heard the sounds of chopping and splitting, and she thought of working to store up supplies for the future. Her sisters never did that. Suddenly she began to weep. It took her by surprise; it was as though she had wanted to do so before but hadn't known how. She looked away from the woman grinding and out of the window toward the increasing dark of night as the tears cascaded down her face onto the table and the floor.

"I never wept for my sisters while I was alone," she thought, "and they ought to be wept for."

"Here," she said to the old woman, "let me grind for you. My arms are younger and stronger than yours."

The old woman didn't say a word. Instead she went to the cupboard and took out some knitting, which she carried to the chair by the fireplace. The old man came in, stretched, and lay down on one of the bunks.

Celia started grinding the mash. It was harder than it looked. She had to pause occasionally to wipe her streaming eyes. She forgot the time and didn't notice when the woman brought another basket of the mash. She forgot the gash in her forehead and the ache behind it.

It grew late and the fire died down. The old woman sat by the fireplace knitting occasionally and dozing occasionally. Celia's arms ached as she turned the crank. Once she stopped and stretched, but an owl's sudden hoot made her start up again; she didn't know why.

So all night long she worked the mill, and the old woman dozed by the fire, which burned lower and lower but never went out. Twice she had to bring new baskets of mash from the door, but the grinding went very slowly, and as the new light from the dawn made the glowing embers seem merely black, there was still only a moderate pile of silken soft flour in the sack.

Celia had stopped weeping for her sisters, and strangely, she didn't feel tired. It was as though she had fulfilled her duty of remorse for them. The old woman shook herself awake. She scraped the stones clean, replenished the fire, and with the new flour made pancakes for breakfast. Celia ate them with the old man. There was little conversation while they ate, but he did remark, "There's a lot of turning in these good cakes," as he put a chunk of butter on his last morsel.

"Yes, and in the churning of the butter, too," his wife replied.

"You know," the man directed this at Celia, "they say this flour warms you three times. First when you pick the acorns, they being so tiny and finicky. Second when you grind them, as you did. And last, when we all eat them.''

"Can you use any kind of acorns and nuts?"

"Oh, we try them all, don't we?" the woman replied. "They're all good, acorns, hazelnuts, beechnuts; the forest is full of good things, as well as dangerous ones like dragons. But why is a stranger like you running around in the forest trying to get herself eaten?"

There was a couple of minutes silence. Then, slowly, Celia began to tell her tale, about her sisters and the fairy godmother, the Prince and the Innkeeper.

"We don't know about such things, at all," the man said.

But the woman said, "We didn't know you were a princess."

And Celia answered, "That's because my helmet dropped off in the stream, and my shield too, with its royal crest."

Then the man said something that made Celia stop and think. "How did the dragon know?"

"What do you mean?"

"Well, dragons do love princesses, but they don't seem to bother us much. Certainly we've never been eaten. Our shack here isn't protected, and it's never been touched. Why do you suppose that is? You say your sister was snatched up out of the courtyard of the inn. But the inn itself has never been harmed, although farmhouses out in the fields are torn to pieces. We don't worry while we work in the forest; we just go out in our old clothes and stay out of their way. If one comes, we stand still, or else move into the trees. Dragons never touch the spruce trees, you know. We are generally dirty from working, and probably smell of the forest; maybe they think we're all some kind of spruce tree. Anyhow, we never worry. But never a princess ventures here who doesn't get eaten.

"So what's different about princesses?"

CELIA still wasn't quite sure, but she had some good ideas. The first thing was not to wear armor at all, for none of the people who lived in the forest did. Next she covered her face and clothes with ashes from the fireplace, including her hair, which was tied up in a kerchief. Then she stuck small spruce branches into her sleeves, collar, belt and everywhere.

The dragons had never touched a spruce tree, although they had destroyed orchards. Perhaps the spruces had a magic of their own, or at least they and the dragons had some kind of agreement. It wasn't, she thought, that she looked very much like a spruce tree, but only that the dragon might not be able to tell that she was a princess, just as the old man had said.

She decided to set a trap for the dragon with her armor, and dropped its many pieces along a narrow path leading off the path she had nearly been caught on. She shined the armor a little to make it pretty visible, and left them — the helmet, hauberk, skirt of tasses, brassart, gauntlets and so on — a little way apart from each other. The narrow path was close pressed by spruce trees, and her plan was to attack the dragon from those trees, where it would have little room to attack *her*.

By the time she was ready, off to one side on her horse, with her lance assembled (its finely ground and shining sharp tip covered with a sprig of spruce), she was breathing hard. "I may have to wait for days," she thought.

But no! Two hours later, near midday, the same dragon came along the wide path and saw the shining pieces of armor leading off to one side. Celia saw the dragon stop and move its head slowly backwards and forwards. The

CHAPTER

8

forest was very quiet and still. Without any noise, smoke began to cloud forth from the dragon's nostrils. Its mouth opened, and it moved steadily down the trail into the trap.

As it moved past Celia, she spurred her horse through the thick spruces and plunged the lance into the dragon right behind its ribs. The shock nearly unseated her, and she wheeled away leaving the lance not very deeply lodged in the beast.

The dragon stopped moving instantly. It started to roar, and the light from the flames jetting from its mouth brightened and dimmed with the sound of the roar. Its head turned sharply to both sides, smashing several spruces as it did so, much to Celia's dismay, for she had been convinced that it would avoid harming the spruces. It twisted its long scaly neck and seemed to inspect the lance in its side. It opened its mouth wider, and the flame just melted away the lance so that it first drooped and then dripped onto the ground.

The dragon looked around, but didn't notice Celia, whose horse was quite still a hundred yards away. Then Celia turned her head and brushed against a branch; her kerchief fell to the ground, and her hair spread out into a halo around her head. Whether the dragon had noticed her before or not, it certainly noticed her then. The roar of the flames became continuous, and it moved directly towards her, bumping against the big trees and smashing the smaller ones.

Celia slapped her horse on the rump, and they raced off round the next bend and along the wide path. Then it happened: the uneven ground caught one of the hooves, and her horse stumbled and fell heavily to one side, pinning her leg underneath the saddle. It didn't hurt much, but she couldn't move.

She looked back, and the roar of the dragon was coming closer. She shivered. "Oh, fairy godmother, I need you again." She hoped that an owl's hoot might mean that her fairy godmother was on her way, but there wasn't much time.

Suddenly a thick but irregularly spaced row of spruce seedlings shot up out of the earth a dozen yards up the path and completely across it. And none too soon, for then the dragon appeared round the bend in the path, leaning to the left and the right as its giant feet propelled it steadily and speedily along. While the trees raced upwards, making an extraordinary kind of fence, their trunks swelled, pushing the earth away in a curled up ridge around each one. Overhead, wide branches thrust out fully needled and wove through each other. Now the path was completely blocked, and the dragon stopped. The smoke and flames passed through the cracks in the magic fence and made Celia cough with their sharpness. But she was safe.

By now the magical trees were very close to each other, and through the slits between them, Celia could see the dragon leaning this way and that, looking for a way through. Its blue eyes gleamed, giving off a blueness so bright that it almost cast shadows. While Celia lay there, her horse wriggled off her and stumbled to its feet. At the base of the nearest tree, something like a door opened, and out hobbled the fairy godmother. She pulled out of her black clothes somewhere a small silver bell. She stood still, looking at Celia expectantly.

Celia rose quickly to her feet. "Thank you very . . ." she started to say, but the fairy godmother quieted her with a finger to her lips. Then she rang the silver bell gently; the roaring stopped, and Celia saw the dragon immediately move away, silently and very fast. The fairy godmother smiled and rang the bell again. The new spruce trees began to ungrow, becoming smaller, pulling the needles into the branches, and the branches into the trunks, and the trunks into the brown earth.

"My dear child," said the fairy godmother in a kind voice, but a little like a school teacher, "dragons are really too big and magically dangerous for you to attack and slay head-on, so to speak. I did tell you that these weren't ordinary dragons. I told you that you have to bring the right weapon. Now that you've seen some real dragons, do you think that lance of yours, or that little sword, no matter how sharp, is the right weapon?"

"I suppose not," said Celia, with as much meekness as she could put together. She felt that her fairy godmother could have been a little more specific before, but she decided that it would be a very poor policy to complain.

"You see, my dear, it's not enough to know that dragons are sympathetic to spruce trees and things with spruce trees in them. These wicked dragons are magic and dangerous and monstrous, indeed. What kind of weapon do you think would be good against dragons?" asked the fairy godmother. It was getting to be more like a classroom every minute.

Celia nearly held up her hand, but just said, "If you please, fairy godmother, since you say that dragons are magic and dangerous and monstrous, I should imagine that I need a magic and dangerous and monstrous weapon to use against them."

She had done it again. The fairy godmother was absolutely delighted and smiled radiantly. "Exactly so, my good child. Now all you have to do is to go and find one." And with this unusual brevity, she smiled again, rang the silver bell, and began to shrink — smile and face and clothes and bell and all.

"Are you going?" asked Celia in some alarm.

"Oh, yes, my dear! But you'll see me again, somewhat higher up; yes, you'll see me again."

It was strange that as she shrank her voice rose rapidly in pitch, so that by the final word "again" it was no more than a squeak. She shrank further, down to a single point of light; then it went out, and she was gone.

Celia couldn't help scowling to herself, but only to herself, for she wasn't sure that an invisibly small fairy godmother couldn't see her — probably she should have been grateful for the cryptic advice. It was all very like the intellectual games her father used to play with her and her sisters at the dinner table when they were much younger.

"Can a man marry his widow's sister?" — that kind of thing. Only here the game seemed impossible, or at least extremely risky. How could she go through the forest looking for magic and dangerous and monstrous weapons to use against magic and dangerous and monstrous dragons? The next dragon would probably eat her while she was looking. Furthermore, she needed time to think. With her father's games, there was always some trick or trap or verbal treachery.

Besides, there wasn't room in the forest — the only magic and dangerous and monstrous things in the forest were dragons.

THEN she knew the answer.

SHE had a lot to do. Late that night, she approached the inn and was surprised to observe the Prime Minister ride up. The Innkeeper greeted him with some deference, and they both went inside. Moving very softly, Celia finished her plans.

THE next morning, in the back room of the inn, the Innkeeper and the Prime Minister were sitting across a table from one another. They were in the room where the money and valuables were stored and where the Innkeeper kept his secret records for the Prime Minister. The Innkeeper was leaning back smoking a pipe. The Prime Minister was studying the books that recorded how many eggs had been collected by the Innkeeper and his stable boys.

"Yes, Innkeeper," he said, "those last two princesses were high-grade maidens all right. Of the nineteen eggs we've found since the first one — Amanda, I think her name was — twelve of them have been grade 1. That means a good bonus."

The Innkeeper smiled evilly. "I'll have to give the boys something extra," he grumbled, "but I'll take it out of taxes. Of course, there's not much, because both the princesses never did pay for their lodging." He frowned. "I should have made them pay in advance."

He thought for a little while, pursing his lips and looking at his pipe, "That's a good idea. I'll make a sign:

PRINCESSES WELCOME
STAY IN OUR SPECIAL IMPERIAL
DRAGON-SLAYER'S SUITE
SPECIAL RATES
RESERVATIONS ACCEPTED.
FREE VICTORY BANQUET.

and then in much smaller letters at the bottom:

KINDLY PAY IN ADVANCE

Yes, that would draw them, I should think."

"Don't jabber on so," said the Prime Minister crossly. It's hard for wicked people not to be cross. "Are there any signs of the third princess? She should have been eaten by now."

"Not yet, but she'll come," the Innkeeper snapped back. "She hasn't been eaten yet; we haven't found a single egg in the last two days." He stood up and looked through the window, which was firmly barred so that nobody could break in and steal the Innkeeper's money.

"What will you do when she gets here? Maybe she knows too much."

"I've still a trick or two up my sleeve," the Innkeeper replied. "Look!" His voice rose in excitement. "She must have passed this way."

He pointed through the bars, and the Prime Minister joined him at the window. Half a mile away, a large dragon was moving steadily along the path towards the inn, with smoke spurting from his nostrils at every breath.

"Yes, he must have smelt her; they never smoke like that unless they're on the track. Oh, it won't come near here. We're perfectly safe. It must be after her, but I don't see her. Here, what's this?"

For the dragon was quite close now and was heading directly for the inn, smoke rhythmically snorting out.

"We've lots of time," the Innkeeper said, although the speed of his movement toward the door belied that. "We'll just nip into the usual clump of spruces; we'll be absolutely safe there."

But when they tried the door, it was locked. The barred window was no help either, and with rapidly rising alarm, they watched the dragon approach.

CELIA, the princess, came out from behind the inn. She had been waiting there for the dragon to follow the trail of armor she had recovered from the previous trap. As soon as she had caught a glimpse of the dragon, she had quietly rushed into the inn and locked all the doors she could see. She mounted her horse and rode hard, right through the courtyard of the inn. In the middle of the night before, she had quietly tied the last and shiniest pieces of her armor onto the roof of the inn.

Half a minute later, the giant beast saw the reflections of its own eyes glistening in the armor; its left foot needed to be lifted just a little higher than its usual pace, and then it came down hard and square on the inn, crushing it absolutely.

Celia was thankful that dragons, like elephants, were too big to be able to run; but they certainly could walk very fast. It was only because her horse was lightly enough loaded that they could keep ahead. They raced into the clearing towards the lone giant spruce tree, just a length or so ahead of the spurting flames and the villainous fangs.

Before dawn that morning, she had built a final trap with the old spruce. An enormous loop of string was attached to a branch which she had pulled down and tied. The loop was tied to a skein that consisted of all her long hair, which was hidden in the low branch.

She aimed her horse breathlessly at the loop hanging from the branches. Then she swerved around the trunk of the spruce as the dragon itself bent beneath that branch and through the loop. As it put its pacing hind legs through as well, Celia, still racing around the tree, slashed the other end of the rope, and the branch snapped up, tightening the loop and dropping the enormous mop of her hair onto the dragon's back, where it sat firmly on the last of the red scales that reached down the beast's spine.

She immediately pulled up her cape to hide what was left of her own hair, and the dragon, reaching around the spruce in pursuit of all that princess hair, saw nearly all of it in one exciting brush on its own tail.

Its odious jaws opened wider and reached forward around the trunk of the tree, finally closing irrevocably on the princess's hair — and its own tail. But its teeth could not be removed except by swallowing, for they pointed back towards its own throat, and its struggles impaled itself deeper and deeper on those tusks.

Celia was, by now, a quarter of a mile away. She watched the dragon circle the tree, unable to free itself, its roar louder than ever, sometimes obscured in flame and smoke, and thumping the ground with an intensity that jolted the ground and nearly unseated her.

THE dragon lay dead. Its jaws were clamped across the thick base of its own tail, its backwards-facing teeth buried deep in its own flesh. Its long tail stretched into the clearing. It had stopped twitching. Out of the dragon's nostrils two thin chimneys of smoke rose straight up into the damp air a dozen feet before curling into a common stream. There was a hideous and unforgettable smell like nothing Celia had ever smelled before. And the whole

beast was wrapped around the trunk of that large spruce tree, dignified and still, pointing to the lowering gray sky.

She stood breathing hard, with her sword in her hand, its tip resting on the ground. "Which part should I cut off?" she thought. "The head is far too large to bring back on my horse or to drag behind it, and I should need not only a cart, but a trailer as well. Perhaps I should take small pieces from here and there."

The first place ought to be the tail, she thought, touching the scab on her forehead. The tail itself was very tough, but her sword finally cut through the last five or six inches, blue and leathery. As she walked up to the swell of the ribs, she noticed that the beast was hot, hotter in fact than could be comfortably touched. She pried off a single red scale from just behind the left front leg — "as near to its wicked heart as possible," she thought. It was the size of a serving platter and just as hot as if it had come from the oven.

She walked around the monstrous jaws, hoping to knock out one of its bright tusks, but it was too late. The jaws were gushing acrid brown and black smoke at an increasing rate. Between the jaws there flickered a gleaming red of flame deep within the entrails. And the dragon consumed itself with its own destructive forces, the smoke and steam from the conflagration rising and twisting up into the low gray clouds through the branches of the giant spruce. The spruce resisted the heat and flames for a while, but then seemed to surrender itself, and the bark and branches flared up. Celia was forced back by the heat, clutching only the tip of the tail and a single red scale. Twenty minutes later the dragon was completely gone, leaving the earth merely a little damp and still steaming from the heat. The bare stump of the tree stood black and charred in the middle. The tip of the tail of the dragon, which Celia had put down on a boulder, had, itself, shriveled, but the scales were still a vivid blue.

"I don't have very much left," said Celia to herself. "I don't have any easy way of proving I have slain a dragon except for these." She looked at the small leathery fragments, one blue, and one red. She stood there, making a far less glorious and regal picture than she had made when she had left the palace. Her splendid long hair was cut raggedly short on all sides, her forehead had a bloody scab in the middle, and everything she wore was muddy and bedraggled.

The clouds overhead turned darker, and Celia noticed that the trees in the clearing were all hissing; the hissing increased until there was a sudden-clap of thunder close by, and then the whole world seemed to relax.

"It's time to be getting back," she thought.

BUT Celia was surprised, indeed, when she took the path back to the ruined inn. When she crossed the small stream, she saw that a small crowd was waiting for her by the road. A cheer rang out. It seemed that a newspaper reporter had been sent to the forest by his enterprising editor — "Get a good picture of Princess What's-Her-Name being devoured, or at least in a good fight. Color, better make it, for the rotogravure section next Sunday. Get a story from the Innkeeper, or make one up. You know." The reporter had arrived just in time to observe Celia slicing off the tip of the tail; he had taken five or six shots and raced back to a telephone.

The crowd consisted of the folk who lived near or in the forest. They cheered Celia again as she approached, and to one side, the reporter was busy snapping photographs. He was very annoyed to learn there was nothing left of the dragon except what Celia had brought with her, and he wished he had stayed longer.

FROM that time on, nobody ever saw another dragon; nobody ever found another sapphire egg. The goblet factory was abandoned and fell into ruin over the years. The goblets could never be replaced, naturally, so that the ones that were left were given to museums and public places. Nobody even bothered to think of the wicked Prime Minister and his evil accomplice.

Gradually people lost their fear of the dark forest, and energetic vacationers would hike through its shady glades and sleep out on its banks of spruce needles. The deer returned, and there were reports that the inn was going to be rebuilt so that hunters could stay there in the autumn.

The abandoned farms around the forest were re-claimed by their old owners, or their children, and new orchards and pastures were started.

WHEN tales are told, and told truly, the tangles must be untangled, the knots unknotted and the loose ends tied up. Life is itself a loose end. In that kingdom by the sea, there was a national celebration over the slaying of the dragon. Three nights later there was a gigantic outdoor feast to celebrate the engagement of the Prince and the princess. It represented both an ending and a beginning.

A great deal of champagne and other wines flowed. Much meat was eaten, and much bread too, not always with the best table manners, but with fervor and happiness. It was a tradition that at such feasts the final course would be spiced puddings, which would be borne out from the kitchens flaming with brandy. Flaming brandy is very pretty to look at, but its light is not very bright. So when the puddings were served, it was the custom to turn out all the lights. That was the signal, in that kingdom, for a set of toasts. Some were public — to the royal family, for example. Some were private — lovers turned to each other and toasted with their eyes and with wordless smiles. Mothers and fathers toasted their families, teachers toasted their students, students their teachers, and every-one, each other.

There was a minute of silence, and then several peo-ple looked up at the sky. A murmur of wonder spread like a tide over the tables. A new constellation had appeared in the sky, around the North Pole, filling an old void with a rambling string of stars that flickered and flared red and blue. This eternal version did not quite surround the Pole Star, but left room for the two bears. Everybody looked up.

"It's the dragons," whispered the multitude. "They've gone. There they are."

"It's a better place for them than my pasture," thought a farmer, "but I still wish I had my old herd."

They were little enough threat now, whirling forever and forever around the peak of heaven. Across the trees the warm and silky wind sounded with a soft roar, a gentle and final echo of the wicked dragons. At the head table the Prince and the princess smiled at each other in the darkness.

"Look," the Prince said. "There are two extra stars in Orion's belt. Two more hunters in the sky. They must be your sisters; I daresay that fairy godmother put them up there. I'm sorry she couldn't come. I'm also sorry I was rude to her a long time ago — it would be nice to see her again."

"Amanda and Belinda will never reach their prey," the princess said soberly, "but they will be always hunting and always admired, as they wanted. Fairy godmother said we might see her again, but higher up, she said."

They looked at each other for an instant, and then together they looked up at the friendly stars. A meteorite flashed in irregular spurts across the sky — hobbling, as it were — leaving a trail of sparks which, for a few seconds, seemed to chatter and gesture to each other. It must have been the fairy godmother herself, playing yet another role and still talking, endlessly.

But nobody else noticed anything at all. And then the puddings came, and the flames and the heady smell of the burning brandy brought everyone back down to earth and life and all good things.

THE END